INCARNATION
YOUTH STUDY BOOK

INCARNATION
REDISCOVERING THE SIGNIFICANCE OF CHRISTMAS

Incarnation: Rediscovering the Significance of Christmas
978-1-7910-0554-2 *Hardcover with jacket*
978-1-7910-0555-9 *eBook*
978-1-7910-0556-6 *Large Print*

Incarnation: DVD
978-1-7910-0559-7

Incarnation: Youth Study Book
978-1-7910-0564-1
978-1-7910-0565-8 eBook

Incarnation: Leader Guide
978-1-7910-0557-3
978-1-7910-0558-0 eBook

**Incarnation:
Children's Leader Guide**
978-1-7910-0553-5

Also by Adam Hamilton

24 Hours That Changed the World

Christianity and World Religions

Christianity's Family Tree

Confronting the Controversies

Creed

Enough

Faithful

Final Words from the Cross

Forgiveness

Half Truths

John

Leading Beyond the Walls

Love to Stay

Making Sense of the Bible

Moses

Not a Silent Night

Revival

*Seeing Gray in a World
of Black and White*

Selling Swimsuits in the Arctic

Simon Peter

Speaking Well

The Call

The Journey

The Walk

The Way

Unafraid

Unleashing the Word

When Christians Get It Wrong

Why?

For more information, visit www.AdamHamilton.com.

ADAM HAMILTON

Author of *The Journey*, *Not a Silent Night*, and *Faithful*

INCARNATION

REDISCOVERING THE SIGNIFICANCE OF CHRISTMAS

YOUTH STUDY BOOK

by Josh Tinley

Abingdon Press | Nashville

Incarnation:
Rediscovering the Significance of Christmas
Youth Study Book

Copyright © 2020 Abingdon Press
All rights reserved.

978-1-7910-0564-1

20 21 22 23 24 25 26 27 28 29—10 9 8 7 6 5 4 3 2 1
MANUFACTURED IN THE UNITED STATES OF AMERICA

CONTENTS

INTRODUCTION

Who is Jesus?

It's a tricky question, but a very important one for those of us who claim to be his followers.

Scripture tells us that Jesus is the promised Messiah. But what does this mean? The word *messiah* literally means "anointed one," but ancient Jewish people had different ideas about what a messiah might look like and what a messiah might do.

The Bible tells us that Jesus is our Savior, and we affirm that Jesus saves us from sin and death. What does this mean and how does it work? We will continue to sin, our sins will still have consequences, and we will still die. However, sin and death no longer have the final say.

The Gospel of Matthew tells us that Jesus is Emmanuel, God with us. Jesus refers to himself as the "light of the world." How does Jesus continue to be with us today and what does his presence mean for the way we live? How does he illuminate our personal lives and our world?

The most common title for Jesus is *Lord*. What does this say about our relationship with Jesus? A *lord* is someone who has authority over an area or community and is responsible for protecting the area and managing its resources. Calling

Jesus *Lord* means submitting to his authority and trusting in his wisdom and guidance.

Christians call Jesus by all of these names because we relate to him in many ways. Regardless of how we understand who Jesus is to us or what role he plays, we know he is always God. In the person of Jesus, God became fully human, lived a fully human life, and died a human death. The word *incarnation*, which means to be made into flesh and blood, describes this concept.

Incarnation is also something we participate in. As God became fully human in the person of Jesus, God's Holy Spirit lives and works through us, Jesus's followers. We reflect the light of Christ and show people God's presence on earth.

As you go through the sessions in this study, you will examine the idea of incarnation and how Christ is our Lord, our Messiah, and our Light. You'll also explore what incarnation means for you and your relationships with other people.

This study includes five sessions:

Session 1: Presidents and Kings

We know that Jesus is God's promised Messiah. But what does this mean? This session looks at what *messiah* meant in Jesus's day and how Jesus defied people's expectations.

Session 2: The Savior and Our Need for Saving

Jesus saves. But from what? Scripture tells us that Jesus delivers us from sin and death. This session examines what that means and how it affects the way we live.

Session 3: Emmanuel in the Midst of a Pandemic

The COVID-19 pandemic of 2020 was a time of fear and anxiety unlike anything many of us had faced before. God's people in scripture faced similarly world-shattering events. In this session, we'll look at how God is present with us in rough times and how God became radically present in the person of Jesus.

Session 4: The Light of the World

Christmas is a time of bright lights and cheer, but we celebrate it during the darkest and dreariest time of year. In this session, we'll discuss how Jesus is the light that breaks through the darkness and how we, as his followers, reflect that light.

Session 5: Falling to Our Knees (Optional)

Christmas doesn't end when we put away the decorations. In this optional concluding session, we'll explore how we carry the truth of Christmas with us throughout the year as we strive to be faithful to our Lord, Jesus Christ. If you choose to use this session, it will be best to hold the group meeting after Christmas, as close as possible to your church's observance of Epiphany.

Using This Resource

This study can be used in Sunday school, during evening youth fellowship gatherings, or as part of a small group or midweek Bible study. There is not a separate youth leader guide for this study. All instructions for leaders and participants are found in this book. The leader of the study could be an adult or one of the student participants.

The five sessions of this study may correspond to the four Sundays of Advent, along with the first Sunday after Christmas. The themes that you will explore are not limited to the Advent and Christmas seasons. This study would be appropriate at any time of year.

All five session plans include

- a brief introduction, summarizing the key themes and learning goals of the session;

- a list of supplies that you will need for each session;
- opening and closing discussion questions and prayers; and
- a variety of discussion questions and learning activities.

The activities in each session, including the opening and closing, should take between fifty and sixty minutes. Every session has at least one optional activity that groups can do if time and interest permit.

Many activities instruct groups to break up into smaller teams. If you have five or fewer participants, do these activities as a single team.

A Note on Virtual Meetings

With some creativity and patience on everyone's part, you can adapt these sessions for virtual, online group study using such platforms as Zoom. Should you want or need to meet virtually:

- Communicate all online meeting details (websites, passwords, beginning time, etc.) to participants well in advance of each session. Create and use an email distribution list, putting your study's name in the subject line so recipients can spot and refer to the email easily. If possible, post contact information for your study (but not each session's log-on information) on your congregation's website.
- If using video in your virtual meeting, be sure you, as leader, are sitting in a well-lit and quiet place in front of a background with few or no distractions. Encourage group participants to do likewise.
- Agree with your members on a group protocol for recognizing who "has the floor." For example, will

participants agree to wait until no one is speaking to answer a question? Will they need to "raise their hand" (physically or digitally) before speaking? Establishing and sticking with some basic ground rules will make your virtual discussions go more smoothly and be more enjoyable and productive.

- Most of the activities listed in this study can be easily adapted for virtual meetings. For those involving recording responses on a whiteboard or large sheet of paper, you can use Zoom's "screen share" feature (or equivalent on a different platform) to display a document where you write down group members' answers. For writing or drawing activities that require supplies, each participant will need to provide their own paper, pens or pencils, and other materials. Be sure to send instructions about the supplies needed ahead of time, so that participants can have them ready before your meeting.

Session 1

PRESIDENTS AND KINGS

For Jewish people in Jesus's day, any talk of a promised king brought to mind one person: King David. For centuries, God's people had been mostly under foreign rule. They were passed from the Babylonians to the Persians to the Greeks and, eventually, to the Romans. Before this turmoil, David and his descendants reigned over Israel, with the time of David and his son Solomon regarded as the golden age. God's people had been in charge of their own kingdom and had successfully defended themselves against powerful neighbors.

Many Jewish people in the first century looked forward to the arrival of a messiah (or anointed one). Most of the people who awaited a messiah expected this person to be the next David. They figured that God's anointed would establish a new kingdom of Israel and drive the Romans out of the land that God had promised to God's people. While the Gospels of Matthew and Luke both tell us that Jesus's family had descended from King David, Jesus didn't bear much resemblance to his famous ancestor. Jesus wasn't a war hero; he didn't command an army; he wasn't interested in living in a palace or sitting on a throne (at least not a throne on earth).

Jesus wasn't the kind of messiah that most people were expecting. Though we call him a king, he wasn't interested in ruling any nation or empire on earth. Even so, Jesus was a leader. Like many leaders in today's world, who win their office through an election, Jesus traveled from place to place delivering a message and making promises. Jesus was "campaigning" for the kingdom of God. He looked forward to a day when God would make all things right and justice would prevail. But he also taught that God's kingdom was already present. We make God's kingdom a reality when we are faithful to Christ's teaching and follow his example of love and sacrifice.

Getting Ready

For this session you will need

- Bibles;
- a whiteboard or large sheets of paper;
- markers;
- pens or pencils; and
- assorted art supplies for making posters.

Opening: Presidents and Kings (10 minutes)

Supplies: a whiteboard or large sheet of paper, markers

As participants arrive, discuss the following question. Write the answers you come up with on a whiteboard or large sheet of paper.

- If you haven't voted in an election already, you likely will be able to sometime in the next few years. When choosing a leader—especially an executive such as a president, governor, or mayor—what qualities are most important to you?

After a few minutes of brainstorming, look over the list you've created.

Then discuss:

- How does your faith influence what you look for in a leader?

A participant should read aloud the following:

> *New Testament writers referred to Jesus as the "King of kings" and "Lord of lords." The magi who visited Jesus as a child referred to him as the "newborn king." When Jesus entered Jerusalem the Sunday before his death, a crowd welcomed him as a long-awaited ruler. Still today, we refer to Jesus as a king, lord, or prince. But what does this mean? How is Jesus similar to and different from the monarchs and heads of state who have overseen nations and empires throughout human history? What does it mean for him to be the "Messiah"? We'll examine these questions and more as we go through this session.*

Anointed One (10 minutes)

Supplies: Bibles, pens or pencils

Discuss:

- What do you think it means to call Jesus the "Messiah"?

A participant should read aloud:

> *The word* messiah, *like the word* Christ, *literally means "anointed one." A messiah was a person anointed, or set apart, by God for a certain purpose.*

Anointing means to pour oil on someone (or something) as a way of signifying that God has set them apart for a specific purpose. Read aloud each of the scriptures below. In teams of three or four, fill in the table by determining which person was anointed and why this person was set apart.

Scripture	Anointed One	Why This Person Was Anointed
Exodus 30:22-32		
1 Samuel 10:1		
1 Samuel 16:1-13		
Isaiah 45:1-2 and Ezra 1:1-4		

After about five minutes, go through the table and make sure that teams agree on who in each scripture is anointed and why. A participant then should read aloud:

> All of these examples are from the Old Testament. Many Jewish people in Jesus's day would have been familiar with the stories of these people. When they heard the word messiah, *they would have thought of people like these.*

Discuss:

- Based on what you read in these scriptures, what do you think Jewish people in Jesus's day would have expected from a messiah?
- In what ways did Jesus meet these expectations?
- How did Jesus contradict these expectations?

David: Israel's Archetypal King
(Optional, 10 minutes)

Supplies: Bibles, pens or pencils

Discuss:

- One of the people we read about in the last activity was King David. In addition to him being anointed by Samuel as Israel's king, what else do you know about David?

A participant should read aloud:

> *David was far from perfect. He is known for his mistakes as much as he is known for his successes. But the descendants of the ancient Israelites considered David their greatest king. He helped establish Israel as a powerful nation, recaptured the ark of the covenant (which held the tablets the Ten Commandments were written on), and protected Israel against its enemies.*

Participants should read aloud 2 Samuel 7:12-16, where the prophet Nathan explains God's covenant with King David.
Discuss:

- What promises does God make to David?

A participant should read aloud:

> *Many of the Jewish people in Jesus's day who believed in a messiah assumed that the messiah would be someone like David who would retake the throne in Israel. Jesus didn't seem to fit the bill. But the Gospel writers found connections between Jesus and his famous ancestor.*

Participants should read aloud the following scriptures:

- Luke 1:26-33
- Luke 2:1-4

Write in the space below ways that these verses from the Gospel of Luke make connections between Jesus and David.

Presidents and Kings (15 minutes)

Supplies: large sheets of paper, markers, assorted art supplies (for making posters)

A participant should read aloud:

> *For much of human history, monarchs such as kings, queens, and emperors ruled over the people in a given region. These monarchs didn't apply or campaign for the job. They either were born into it or took the throne after prevailing in battle or defeating a rival. Nowadays, most major political leaders spend several months campaigning in the hopes that citizens will elect them. Some leaders spend almost as much time on the campaign trail as they do in office. Jesus didn't have to campaign for the role of Messiah, but he did have to show people why he was God's anointed.*

Divide into teams of three or four. Each team should imagine that they're running a campaign for Jesus and make a campaign poster. The poster should make the case that Jesus is God's promised Messiah. It could include reasons why people might see Jesus as the Messiah; it also could respond to objections that people might have. Some examples of each are below.

Reasons people might see Jesus as the Messiah

- Descendant of King David
- Born in Bethlehem (David's city)
- Able to feed large crowds with limited resources
- Able to heal the sick and injured

Reasons people might object to Jesus as the Messiah

- Grew up in Nazareth (small town in the middle of nowhere)
- Family was not wealthy or powerful
- Clashed with religious leaders
- No military experience

Allow several minutes to work on posters. Then each team should present its poster to the group.

A participant then should read aloud:

> *While Jesus was a descendant of David, born in Bethlehem, and performed amazing miracles, he is not the Messiah for any of these reasons. He is the Messiah because of the sacrifice he made on our behalf, because of the hope we have in his resurrection, and because of the relationship he continues to have with us.*

Jesus's Anointing and Coronation (10 minutes)

Supplies: Bibles, dictionary

Discuss:

- What does it mean to "anoint" someone?

19

Look up the word *anoint* in a dictionary. Discuss:

- What, if anything, surprises you about this definition?
- Who is usually responsible for anointing people?
- What do these people use to anoint?

Jesus wasn't anointed by a priest or a king, but he was anointed.

Divide into three teams. Have each team read one of the following scriptures:

- Luke 7:36-48
- Matthew 26:6-13
- John 12:1-11

After a minute or so, each team should summarize its scripture passage for the group.

Discuss:

- What are some of the similarities you see among these scriptures?
- What are some things that seem unique to your team's scripture?
- What sacrifices were made in these scriptures?
- What did you notice about the people who anointed Jesus in these scriptures? Why might it be significant that these people are anointing Jesus?

The Return and Final Triumph of the King (15 minutes)

Supplies: Bibles, paper, markers or colored pencils, whiteboard or large sheets of paper

A participant should read aloud:

As Jesus's followers, we eagerly await God's kingdom. Often, we think of God's kingdom as something we'll experience when Christ returns in the future. But there's more to it.

A participant should read aloud Luke 17:20-21.
Discuss:

- What does Jesus say, in this scripture, about God's kingdom?

Another participant should read aloud Matthew 6:9-13 (the Lord's Prayer).
Discuss:

- What do you think Jesus means when he says, "Your kingdom come. Your will be done, on earth as it is in heaven" (v. 10)?

God's kingdom is not something we have to wait for. We can make God's kingdom a reality here and now through our words, actions, and relationships.

In God's kingdom, God—the one true King—makes all things right. Think about what God's kingdom should look like. What would the world look like if there were no more hate or injustice? Take a few minutes to write or draw on a sheet of paper your vision for God's kingdom.

After a few minutes, present to one another your visions of God's kingdom. Discuss the similarities among your visions as well as what was unique to one person's vision.

We live in a world that is far from perfect—a world that still experiences suffering, violence, and oppression. But Jesus tells us that God's kingdom is here, among us.

Divide a whiteboard or large sheet of paper into two columns.

As a group, brainstorm examples of how you see God's kingdom in the world right now. Write these in the first column. This could include people or groups who are working to bring hope and fight injustice, people and groups who have found the strength to forgive one another, or people who have been healed and made whole.

Then brainstorm ways that you, as individuals or as a group, could make God's kingdom a reality. This might include acts of kindness and compassion, efforts to respond to suffering or injustice in your community, or efforts to restore broken relationships through forgiveness.

Closing (5–10 minutes)

Discuss:

- What is one thing you learned during our time together that you didn't know before?
- What is one thing that you will do in the coming week as a result of what we learned or discussed? (Think especially about the examples you listed during the final activity.)

Then close with the following prayer or one of your choosing:

Lord, thank you for the time we've had together today to learn from scripture and one another. Open our eyes to all the ways that you are at work in our world today. Open our hearts to all the ways we can participate in the work of your kingdom. We pray all these things in the name of Christ, our Messiah. Amen.

Session 2

THE SAVIOR AND OUR NEED FOR SAVING

The name *Jesus* is the English version of the Greek version of Jesus's actual Hebrew name, *Yeshua* or *Yehoshua*, a name that literally means "to save" or "to deliver." Scripture teaches us that Jesus is our Savior. What does this mean? What does Jesus save us from?

The short answer is that Jesus saves us from sin and death. How that happens and what it means for us is a bit more complicated. Jesus, through his death on the cross, forgives and atones for our sins. This doesn't mean that we won't sin anymore or that our sins won't have consequences. Struggling with sin is part of being human. The good news is that Jesus sets an example and gives us a path to follow. When we wander off of that path (and we will), Jesus—through his teaching, and the wisdom and example of his followers—guides us and strengthens us so that we can get back on track.

Jesus died for our sins, but he also was resurrected, defeating death. Like Jesus, we all will die a human death. But because of Jesus we know that death doesn't get the last word.

Jesus promises that we, too, will experience resurrection. This eternal life that Jesus promises isn't something we have to wait for. Now, in this life, we can claim the hope that we have through Jesus and live as people who do not fear death.

Getting Ready

For this session you will need

- Bibles;
- a whiteboard or large sheets of paper;
- markers;
- pens or pencils; and
- a timer.

Opening: You Saved Me (5–10 minutes)

As participants arrive, everyone should think of a situation where someone saved you. This situation doesn't need to involve someone saving your life. It could involve a friend letting you borrow something urgent, a teacher allowing you extra time to finish an assignment, or a stranger lending you a dollar or two when you were short.

When most people are present, invite each person to talk about the situation in which he or she was saved.

After this discussion, open with the following prayer or one of your choosing:

God our Savior, thank you for bringing us back together for this time of learning and discussion. Bless our time, and open our hearts and minds to the message that you have for us today.

What Jesus Saves Us from (5 minutes)

Supplies: a whiteboard or large sheet of paper, markers

Discuss:

- What comes to mind when you hear the phrase, "Jesus saves"?

Work together to brainstorm any words or phrases that come to mind when you think of salvation or being saved. This could include things we are saved from, things we are saved for, and ways that we claim salvation. List these on a whiteboard or large sheet of paper.

Then discuss:

- What questions do you have about salvation or what it means to be saved?

A participant should read aloud the following:

> *Jesus's name in Hebrew—Yeshua or Yehoshua— literally means "to save" or "to deliver." Saving, or salvation, is an important part of who Jesus is and what he came to do.*

Saved from Sin (15 minutes)

Supplies: Bibles, large sheets of paper, markers, whiteboard

A participant should read aloud Matthew 1:18-21. Discuss:

- According to the angel, what will Jesus do?

A participant should read aloud the following:

> *Scripture tells us that Jesus is our Savior, sent to save us from sin. The Hebrew and Greek words most commonly translated as sin—hata in Hebrew and hamartia in Greek—literally mean to "miss the mark" or "stray from the path."*

Divide into teams of three or four. If possible, create teams of people who have similar interests (a team of musicians, a team of athletes, a team of students interested in math and science, and so on).

Each team should come up with a goal related to its members' interest. (For example, qualifying for a championship track or swim meet, creating an online video and getting a certain number of views, or getting a certain score on a portion of the ACT or SAT.)

Teams should take about one minute to determine a goal. They should write this at the top of a large sheet of paper. Beneath this title teams should split their papers into two columns. Label the first column "Path." Teams then should take another minute to name steps that a person would need to take to meet this goal and list these steps under "Path."

Teams should label the second column "Diversions." They then should spend about two minutes discussing things that would divert them from their path. For example, "skipping practice" or "eating a lot of junk food" could keep someone from the goal of qualifying for a big track or swim meet; giving into the temptation to spend hours playing video games or binging TV shows could prevent someone from adequately preparing for an ACT or SAT.

Each team then should present its work to the others, briefly explaining its chosen goal, its path, and its possible diversions.

A participant then should read aloud:

> *As followers of Christ, our goal is to be like Jesus. There are lots of ways that we work toward this goal. We pray, read and study scripture, participate in worship, perform acts of kindness and justice, and so forth. No matter how devoted we are to this goal, we all wander off the path. One way to understand sin is to identify it as anything that deters us from this path.*

Take a minute to brainstorm sins and list them on a whiteboard or large sheet of paper. For this activity, don't focus on specific sins. Instead, think of types of sin. For instance: "selfishness" or "hatred."

After one minute, discuss:

- How do each of the items on our list cause us to stray from the path of following Jesus?

Wrestling with the Devil (Optional, 15 minutes)

Supplies: Bibles

A participant should read aloud the following:

> *Jesus delivers us from our sins through his sacrifice on the cross. But he also saves us from sin by giving us the strength to fight it.*

Pair off. (If you have an odd number of participants, an adult leader can be part of one pair.) Each pair should thumb-wrestle. After the match, the winner should then pair off with the winner of another match; the loser should pair with the loser of another match. Continue until everyone has participated in four or five matches.

A participant then should read aloud the following:

> *Resisting sin and staying on the path of discipleship is a struggle. We wrestle with temptation and doubt as we strive to focus on God's will. One way that scripture talks about our fight with sin is as a struggle against the devil.*

Then a participant should read aloud the following scriptures:

- Ephesians 6:10-17
- James 4:7-10

27

Discuss:

- What do these scriptures say about our struggle against sin?
- How, according to these Scriptures, do we "resist the devil" or "stand against the tricks of the devil"?

Forgiveness of Sins (10–15 minutes)

Supplies: Bibles, whiteboard or large sheet of paper, markers

Divide a whiteboard or large sheet of paper into two columns. Label one "Forgiveness Is"; label the other "Forgiveness Is Not."

List in the first column examples of what forgiveness is. Think about what forgiveness means, what happens to the person being forgiven, and what happens to the person doing the forgiving.

Do this for about one minute. Then list in the second column examples of what forgiveness is not. Think about things that don't happen or change just because someone has been forgiven or has forgiven someone else.

After another minute, discuss:

- What happens to a person when he or she forgives someone else? How does he or she change?
- What happens to a person when he or she is forgiven? How does he or she change?

A participant then should read aloud the following:

Scripture tells us that Jesus died for the forgiveness of our sins. This does not mean that our mistakes will not have consequences. It does, however, mean that our sins will not be held against us and that we have an opportunity to change and grow in our relationship with Christ.

Participants should read aloud each of the following scriptures. For each scripture, discuss:

- What does this scripture say about Jesus's forgiveness of our sins?

Scriptures

- Romans 5:6-9
- Ephesians 1:7-8
- Colossians 1:13-14

Christ's Salvation and Our Existential Crises (Optional, 10 minutes)

Supplies: a timer

Everyone should take exactly one minute (set a timer) to think about their answer to the question, "What is the meaning of life?" (or "What is the point or purpose of life?")

When the timer runs out, go around the room and have each person say, in twenty seconds or less, their answer to the question.

Humans have struggled with this question for millennia. While it's a tough question for anyone, as Christians, we can look to our faith for answers.

Divide into three teams. Each team should read one of the following scriptures and answer the question:

- What does this scripture teach us about the meaning and purpose of our lives?

Scriptures

- Romans 6:8-14
- Galatians 5:16, 22-26
- 1 Thessalonians 5:15-24

You Are Loved (10 minutes)

A participant should read aloud the following:

> *Jesus's birth was an act of love. God came to earth in the person of Jesus to live as a human being and to be in relationship with humanity. In the person of Jesus, out of love, God made the ultimate sacrifice on our behalf. God wants us to know that we are loved. But not everyone knows or feels this love.*

Brainstorm and list on a whiteboard or large sheet of paper circumstances or events that might cause people not to feel God's love. Examples might include: losing a loved one, suffering from a natural disaster, and so on. Don't name specific people.

After a couple minutes, discuss:

- How have people shown you that you were loved during difficult times?

As a group, go through the items you listed. For each one, identify at least one way you could let people facing these circumstances know that they are loved. This could involve a kind word and a smile, providing for their basic needs, lending a listening ear, or offering assistance.

Once you've gone through the list and come up with various ways to show God's love, discuss:

- In what ways can you show God's love to someone else—especially someone going through difficult circumstances—this week?

Saved from Death (5–10 minutes)

Supplies: Bibles

A participant should read aloud John 11:17-27.

Discuss:

- Who has died in this scripture?
- Who are Mary and Martha? (What is their relationship to the person who has died?)
- How does Martha respond when Jesus tells her that her brother will "rise again" (v. 23)?
- What do you think Jesus means when he refers to himself as "the resurrection and the life" (v. 25)?
- What do you think Jesus means when he says that people "even though they die, will live" (v. 25)?

A participant should read aloud:

In these verses, Jesus's friend Lazarus has died. After this conversation with Mary and Martha, Jesus brings Lazarus back to life. Lazarus, like other people that Jesus brought back to life in the Gospels, would eventually die again, as all humans do. The "resurrection" Jesus was talking about was something different, something more.

Discuss:

- How is resurrection different from simply coming back to life?
- How does (or how should) Jesus's promise of resurrection affect how we live—our behaviors and our attitudes—every day?

Closing (5–10 minutes)

Discuss:

- What is one thing you learned during our time together that you didn't know before?

- What is one thing that you will do in the coming week as a result of what we learned or discussed? (Think especially about the examples you listed during the final activity.)

Then close with the following prayer or one of your choosing:

Lord of salvation, thank you for the time we've had together today to learn from scripture and one another about how you, in and through Jesus Christ, save us from sin and death. Open our hearts and minds to the hope that we have through our relationship with you, and equip us to show your love to everyone we encounter.

Session 3

EMMANUEL IN THE MIDST OF A PANDEMIC

The COVID-19 pandemic of 2020 was unlike anything most of us had experienced in our lifetimes. Hundreds of thousands of people suffered from a highly contagious disease that forced us to change our lifestyles completely. It had been a scary time, and for much of it, we had no idea of when or how it would end.

The story of God's people in scripture includes several devastating events. The kingdom of Israel, which had prospered under David and Solomon, split into two smaller kingdoms, Israel and Judah. They were sometimes at odds with each other. Divided, the two kingdoms struggled to defend themselves against their powerful neighbors. While God's people endured turmoil for centuries, they never were without hope. God sent prophets to assure the people that God would deliver them from enemies, to call them back to the covenant God had made with them, to speak out against injustice and oppression, and to remind the people that God loved them and had big plans for them.

Eventually, God got personal. At a time when God's people were under Roman rule and there was a great deal of unrest, God became human and lived among God's people as Jesus of Nazareth. In Jesus, God experienced life as a human, with all of the pain and temptation that went along with it. By becoming fully human—God incarnated in human flesh—Christ not only was able to make the ultimate sacrifice on our behalf, but he also was able to sympathize with the struggles that human beings deal with.

Getting Ready

For this session you will need

- Bibles;
- a whiteboard or large sheets of paper;
- markers;
- pens or pencils;
- slips of paper; and
- Bibles or Bible dictionaries with a map of the divided kingdoms of Israel and Judah

Opening: Quarantine Days (10 minutes)

As participants arrive, talk about your experiences in quarantine in response to the COVID-19 pandemic. You can discuss some or all of the following questions:

- How did your life change as a result of the pandemic?
- What challenges have you faced as a result of the pandemic that you hadn't faced before?
- How did you stay connected to your church community during the quarantine? How did you pray and worship?
- How did you see God at work in the ways that people in

your community—or elsewhere in the world—responded to the pandemic?

• When, many years from now, you look back on this event, what do you think you will remember most?

A participant should read aloud the following:

> *The 2020 COVID-19 pandemic affected just about everyone. Most of us, at some point during the pandemic, experienced fear or anxiety or had to change the way that we went about our day-to-day lives. We see similar world-shattering events in scripture. God's people dealt with invasions from powerful foreign empires that would destroy their cities, place restrictions on their religious practices, and send some of the people into exile in foreign lands, among other things. Through it all, God sent prophets to show people that there was hope for the future and that God was still in charge.*

Open with this prayer or one of your choosing:

God of good times and bad, thank you for bringing us back together for this time of learning and discussion. Bless our time and open our hearts and minds to the message that you have for us today.

Background: A Kingdom Divided (Optional, 5–10 minutes)

Supplies: Bibles, a map of the divided kingdoms of Israel and Judah (commonly found in study Bibles or Bible dictionaries, or online)

Ahead of time, find a study Bible, Bible dictionary, or website with a map of the divided kingdoms of Israel and Judah. (Many Bibles that have a map section will have one of these maps. If possible, make sure that each person has a map that he or she can look at. One great website is https://www.bibleodyssey.org /tools/map-gallery/i/map-israel-and-judah).

A participant should read aloud the following:

> *Ancient Israel included twelve tribes. Each tribe traced its ancestry to one of the sons of Jacob in the Book of Genesis. After settling the Promised Land and fending off many powerful enemies under the leadership of prophets called judges, the Israelites established a kingdom. But after the death of Israel's third king, Solomon, the kingdom split. The largest tribe, Judah, along with the tribe of Benjamin, formed the kingdom of Judah. The other ten tribes continued to call themselves the kingdom of Israel.*

Identify the kingdoms of Israel and Judah on the maps; then discuss:

- Which kingdom is in the north? Which is in the south?
- In which of the kingdoms is the city of Jerusalem?

Isaiah's Prophecy (5–10 minutes)

Have a participant read aloud Matthew 1:22-23. In verse 23, Matthew quotes the Old Testament, Isaiah 7:14.

Have another participant read aloud Isaiah 7:13-17.

A participant should read aloud the following:

> *When Isaiah wrote these verses, he didn't have Jesus in mind. He was speaking to Ahaz, the king of Judah, at a time when Judah was under attack from Israel and another nation called Aram. He wrote of a child named* Immanuel, *which literally means "God with us." By the time Immanuel was old enough to "refuse the evil and choose the good" (v.16), Israel and Aram would no longer be a threat.*

Discuss:

- At what age, do you think, is someone old enough to "refuse the evil and choose the good"?
- Why is the child's name, *Immanuel*, important? What does *Immanuel* mean and how does that name relate to what Isaiah is talking about?
- Why do you think the Gospel of Matthew referred to this story when telling the story of Jesus's birth?
- How was Jesus similar to Immanuel in Isaiah 7?

The Incarnation (15 minutes)

Supplies: slips of paper, pen or pencils

Distribute slips of paper. Each person should write on a slip of paper a definition of the word *incarnation*. It is okay if not everyone knows or understands the meaning of the word. (In fact, it's probably better if some people do not.)

One person, maybe an adult leader, should look up a dictionary definition of *incarnation* and write it on a slip of paper. This person should collect the slips, shuffle them up, and read them one at a time.

After everyone has heard each definition once, the person with the slips of paper should read aloud the definitions one more time. This time, participants should vote on which definition they think comes from the dictionary. See which person's definition gets the most votes as the dictionary definition. (Consider awarding a small prize to the winner.)

Then discuss:

- How does the word *incarnation* apply to Jesus?

To get a better understanding of the meaning of incarnation, discuss:

- What movies and television shows can you think of in which God is a character?
- How is God portrayed in these shows and movies? (Focus less on what God looks and sounds like and more on God's personality and behavior.)

A participant should read aloud the following:

> *For centuries, writers and artists have imagined God as a human being. But because of incarnation, we don't have to imagine. We know that God is three persons: Father, Son, and Holy Spirit. Through Jesus, God lived among us as a human being. Jesus gives us our clearest picture of who God is and what matters to God.*

A participant should read aloud John 1:1-5, 14.
Then a participant should read aloud the following:

> *These verses tell us that God's Word, Jesus Christ, who has been with God since the beginning, became "flesh," and lived on earth as a human being.*

Discuss:

- How does the fact that God lived as a human being— with all the temptations and struggles that humans experience—affect our relationship with God?
- How might our relationship with God be different if God hadn't experienced life as a human?

Everyone should imagine that he or she must describe Jesus in twenty seconds or less. Allow a minute or two for everyone to think about his or her twenty-second description. Then invite each person to give his or her description. (Set a timer for twenty seconds for each one.)

Discuss:

- What similarities did you notice in our descriptions?
- What words and phrases did you hear in other people's descriptions that you wouldn't have thought of on your own?
- We believe that Jesus is our clearest picture of what God is like. Based on these descriptions of Jesus, what do we know about God?

Our Mission—to Incarnate the Love of God (10–15 minutes)

Supplies: whiteboard or large sheet of paper, markers

Think back to everyone's descriptions of Jesus from the previous activity. Brainstorm any words or phrases that you remember people using to describe Jesus. List these on a whiteboard or large sheet of paper.

Look over your list. Reflect on people you know who have some of these same qualities that you've attributed to Jesus. Write the names of these people, and their Christlike qualities, below.

Take a few minutes to work. Then go around the room. Each person should name one person he or she listed and how this person is like Jesus. If time permits, go around the room additional times.

One of Jesus's most significant qualities is sacrifice. Take a couple of minutes to think of people you know who have made extraordinary sacrifices for you, for your community, or for people elsewhere in the world. These could be people who sacrificed their lives, but it also could be people who sacrificed their time, their safety, their money, or their well-being. List these people, and the sacrifices they made, below. (It is okay if you list some of the people you already listed above.)

Go around the room again. Each person should name one person he or she listed and the sacrifice this person made. (Again, if time permits, go around the room more than once.)

Now think of how you can incarnate God's love. How can you be like Jesus in the coming week? Commit to one specific way that you will be like Jesus this week and describe your commitment below. Again, be specific. (Instead of writing, "I will be kind," say, "I will go out of my way to do at least one act of kindness each day," or "When I'm tempted to say something unkind, I will instead say a prayer for the person I was tempted to be unkind to.")

After a couple of minutes, allow volunteers to talk about their commitments for the week.

Closing (5–10 minutes)

Discuss:

- What is one thing you learned during our time together that you didn't know before?
- What is one thing that you will do in the coming week as a result of what we learned or discussed? (Think especially about the examples you listed during the final activity.)

Then close with the following prayer or one of your choosing:

Lord, thank you again for this time we've had to learn from scripture and from one another. Thank you for living among us in the person of Jesus to better understand our temptations and struggles, and to set an example for how we should live. Thank you for all of the Christlike people in our lives and in our communities who have shown us your love and sacrifice. Equip and empower us to be incarnations of your love. We pray all these things in Jesus's name. Amen.

Session 4

THE LIGHT OF THE WORLD

Our culture celebrates Christmas as a time of bright lights and great joy. Yet, at least in the northern hemisphere, Christmas falls during the darkest, coldest, bleakest time of year. This is not because Jesus just happened to be born in late December. Scripture doesn't tell us the time of year when Jesus was born. December 25 was chosen because it is close to the winter solstice. On this date (usually December 21 or 22), the earth is tilted so that people in the northern hemisphere receive less daylight than on any other day of the year. It is the shortest day and the longest night. But, after the winter solstice, the days get longer. Bit by bit, the light overcomes the darkness.

As we explored in the previous session, Jesus was born during a dark time for God's people. The opening chapter of John's Gospel describes Christ as the "light." "The light shines in the darkness," John writes, "and the darkness did not overcome it" (John 1:5). Later in John, Jesus describes himself as "the light of the world" and promises that his followers won't "walk in darkness" (John 8:12).

Jesus's followers don't walk in darkness because we reflect the light of Jesus. Though Christ no longer walks the earth as a human being, he is still present. Jesus is most visible in the world today through the lives and actions of his disciples. When we follow Jesus's examples and teaching, we become Christ's presence on earth.

Getting Ready

For this session you will need

- Bibles;
- a whiteboard or large sheets of paper;
- markers;
- pens or pencils; and
- a candle.

Opening: Light in the Darkness (5–10 minutes)

As participants gather, talk about Christmas light displays. Discuss the following questions:

- What is the most impressive Christmas light display you've seen?
- What type of Christmas light display do you prefer? Do you prefer simple strands of lights in a single color? Do you prefer multicolored lights that cover everything? Do you like figurines and other decorations?
- Does your family put up outdoor lights for Christmas? If so, is it worth the effort? Why or why not?
- How does seeing Christmas lights during the Advent season affect your mood (if at all)?

Open with the following prayer or one of your choosing:

God of light, thank you for bringing us back together for this time of learning and discussion. Bless our time and open our hearts and minds to the message that you have for us today.

The Longest Night (Optional, 5–10 minutes)

Supplies: Bibles, a device with internet access (optional)

Discuss:

- What is the longest night of the year? (In other words, what is the shortest day? As necessary, do research on an electronic device to make sure that you have the correct date.)
- How close is this longest night to our celebration of Christmas?
- Once this longest night passes, what will happen to the lengths of the days and nights?

A participant should read aloud the following:

Scripture doesn't tell us the date or time of year of Jesus's birth. While people have made guesses based on the little information we have, there is no evidence that he was born on or around December 25. When Christians established Christmas as a holiday in the fourth century, they picked a date that was close to the winter solstice—the day of the year with the least light. The Christmas season is the darkest time of year. But it's also the time of the year when light begins to overcome darkness and the days start getting longer.

Another participant should read aloud John 1:9-13. Discuss:

- Who is the "light" in these verses?
- What does the light do?

Darkness and Light in Scripture (10 minutes)

Supplies: Bibles

Divide into teams of three or four. Assign one or more of the following scriptures to each team. Every team should read its assigned scriptures and be prepared to answer the following question.

- What do these verses say about light, darkness, and/or the relationship between light and darkness?

Scriptures

- Genesis 1:1-5
- John 9:1-5
- Romans 13:11-14
- 2 Corinthians 4:5-6
- 1 John 2:7-11
- Revelation 22:1-5

Discuss:

- "Darkness" in scripture doesn't always refer to literal darkness. What else does "darkness" represent in these scriptures?
- What about light? What does light represent in these scriptures?

Light Incarnate (10–15 minutes)

Supplies: Bibles, pens or pencils

A participant should read aloud:

As we've seen, one way that light is used in scripture is as a description of Jesus. Jesus is the "light" of the world. As we discussed in the previous session, Jesus sets an example for us to follow. Like Jesus, we can bring light into the world.

Reflect on a time in your life when you were hurting or struggling and someone gave you hope or peace. This person might have been a reminder that you were loved and cared for; this person might have given you the strength and courage to keep going; or this person might have helped put things into perspective. Write about this time in your life and this person below.

After everyone has had a few minutes to think and write, allow volunteers to talk about what they wrote.

Then a participant should read aloud Mark 6:33-38.

Discuss:

- What need do Jesus's disciples identify in these verses?
- What does Jesus instruct the disciples to do?
- How do the disciples respond?

47

A participant should read aloud the following:

When the disciples mention that there are a lot of people who need to eat, Jesus doesn't immediately solve the problem. Instead, he tells his disciples to act. Jesus is the Light of the world, but he calls on us to reflect his light to make it visible to everyone we encounter.

The Word of God (5–10 minutes)

Supplies: Bibles, pens or pencils

Discuss:

- What comes to mind when you hear the phrase "Word of God"?

A participant should read aloud John 1:1-5. (These verses should sound familiar since you read them in a previous session.)
Discuss:

- According to these verses, who or what is the "Word" of God?

The Greek word for *word* is translated as *logos*.
Discuss:

- Look at the word *logos*. What English words do you think it is related to?

A participant should read aloud the following:

The Greek word logos *is translated as "word," but it means more than that. Logos* refers to wisdom, order, and logic. The "Word," or logos, of God is what gives creation its meaning and structure.*

Masterpieces (Optional, 10 minutes)

God's Word is the ultimate expression of God that helps us fully understand God and God's will. To better understand God's relationship to God's Word, think about your favorite artist. This can be a musician, an author, a screenwriter, a director, a playwright, a composer, a painter, or a sculptor. Write this person's name below:

Then think about this person's work. What would you consider this person's masterpiece—his or her greatest work of art? Write this below.

Now think about what the piece of art you identified above tells you about the artist. What does it say about the person's values and beliefs? What does it say about their influences? What does it say about the artist's work ethic or creative process? How is the art an expression of the artist's love? Describe this below.

After everyone has had several minutes to work through these questions, allow volunteers to talk about their artists, works of art, and what the art says about the artist.

Then discuss:

- What does God's Word, Christ, tell us about God?
- How is God's Word an expression of God's love?

Walking in and Sharing the Light (10 minutes)

Supplies: whiteboard or large sheet of paper, marker, a candle, matches or lighter

As a group, identify all the ways that your congregation and youth ministry use candles in worship and other church activities. List these on a whiteboard or large sheet of paper.

Discuss:

- What do you think is the significance of all these candles?

Candles represent not only the light of Christ, but also the light that each one of us takes into the world.

Participants should take a couple minutes to think of ways that any person—not just himself or herself—can reflect Christ's light in the world. Think of small ways that someone can show others God's love, peace, and compassion during his or her day-to-day life.

After everyone has had some time to think, gather in a circle.

One person should light a candle. This person should say, "I challenge you to reflect Christ's light in the world by…" He or she should finish the sentence with one way that a person could reflect the light of Christ. Then this person should pass the candle to his or her left. The next person should repeat the same statement with a different challenge.

Continue until the candle has made its way all the way around the circle.

Closing (5–10 minutes)

Discuss:

- What is one thing you learned during our time together that you didn't know before?
- What is one thing that you will do in the coming week as a result of what we learned or discussed? (Think especially about the examples you listed during the final activity.)

Then close with the following prayer or one of your choosing:

Lord of light, thank you again for this time we've had to learn from scripture and from one another. Equip us and empower us to reflect the light of Christ, so that everyone we encounter might experience your love, peace, and compassion. We pray all these things in Jesus's name. Amen.

Session 5

FALLING TO OUR KNEES
(OPTIONAL)

In our culture, the Christmas season begins when businesses and cities put up their decorations (usually sometime in November) and continues until we all put away our decorations and return to our normal routine (usually right after New Year's Day). But on the Christian calendar, the Christmas season begins on Christmas Eve. Everything leading up to Christmas is Advent. Christmas continues for twelve days (like the song) until January 6, a day we call the Epiphany.

The Epiphany is the date when we remember the visit of the magi, or wise men. The magi traveled in search of a newly born "king of the Jews," which was a shock to the current king, Herod the Great. When they found the Christ Child, they brought three gifts. Traditionally, these three gifts represent three ways we understand Jesus. The gift of gold represents Jesus's royalty and our belief in Jesus as a new kind of king. The gift of frankincense represents Jesus's divinity. The smoke from burning incense symbolized prayers rising to God in heaven. We know that Jesus, though he was human, is also fully God. The gift of myrrh represents Jesus's humanity. Jesus lived as a human being and died a human death. Myrrh was used for preparing bodies for burial.

The magi regarded Jesus as a king, but we often use another word to recognize Jesus's royalty and authority: *Lord*. A *lord* is someone who has authority over a particular area. The lord, or lady, is responsible for the distribution of food and other resources and protection of those in his or her care. When we call Jesus, *Lord*, we confess that he is our authority, and that we serve him and depend on him for guidance and protection. Calling Jesus—instead of earthly leaders and powers—our Lord means being faithful to him by following his teaching and caring for his people.

Getting Ready

For this session you will need

- Bibles;
- a whiteboard or large sheets of paper;
- markers; and
- pens or pencils.

Opening: Season's End? (5–10 minutes)

As participants arrive, talk about when your yearly Christmas celebrations end. Discuss questions such as:

- What do you think is the official end of the Christmas season?
- What is the latest you've celebrated Christmas with friends or family?

- When do you and your family take down your Christmas decorations?
- At what point does it seem weird to drive by houses that still have Christmas decorations up or to walk into stores that are still decorated for Christmas?

When most people are present, a participant should read aloud the following:

> *On the church calendar, the Christmas season starts on Christmas Eve. Everything leading up to Christmas is part of Advent. Christmas continues for twelve days, just like the song says. Twelve days after Christmas, on January 6, is Epiphany—the date when we celebrate the visit of the magi, or wise men. So, Christmas officially ends on January 6. But in this session, we'll look at how to carry the lessons of Christmas with us through the year.*

Open with the following prayer or one of your choosing:

God of all seasons, thank you for bringing us back together for this time of learning and discussion. Bless our time and open our hearts and minds to the message that you have for us today.

The Dedication of Jesus at the Temple (10–15 minutes)

Supplies: Bibles

Discuss:

- What in your life have you waited the longest for?
- Why were you so eager for this to happen?
- Did the thing you were waiting for live up to your expectations? Why or why not?

A participant should read aloud the following:

On the eighth day after his birth, Jesus's parents, following Jewish tradition, presented Jesus in the temple. When they got there, they met a couple of people who had been waiting.

Participants should read aloud Luke 2:25-35.
Discuss:

- Who is Simeon?
- What is Simeon waiting for?
- What does Simeon tell Mary and Joseph about Jesus?

Then a participant should read aloud Luke 2:36-38.
Discuss:

- Who is Anna?
- How does she respond to seeing Jesus and his family?
- How is Anna's response similar to and different from Simeon's?

A participant should read aloud the following:

Even though Simeon prayed that God could let him "go in peace," he spoke about what Jesus would mean for the future of God's people. Anna, who'd been waiting in the temple for decades, was excited about what the future had in store. Both Anna and Simeon had been eagerly waiting for Christmas. They understood that when Jesus finally arrived, he brought with him a new beginning.

The Visit of the Magi (10 minutes)

Supplies: Bibles, a whiteboard or large sheet of paper, marker

Brainstorm and list on a whiteboard or large sheet of paper everything you know about the visit of the magi.

After a couple minutes of brainstorming, participants should read aloud the story of the magi from Matthew 2:1-12.

Discuss:

- Is there anything you remembered about the magi that turned out to be incorrect? If so, what?
- What details in this story were you unaware of? What, if anything, surprised you in this story?
- What three gifts did the magi bring to Jesus?
- Most people are familiar with gold. What do you know about the other two gifts, frankincense and myrrh?

A participant should read aloud the following:

Traditionally, the magi's gold represents Christ's royalty, because gold is associated with kings. Frankincense is a type of incense. When burned, it creates smoke that represents prayers going up to God in heaven. For this reason, frankincense represents Christ's divinity, or the truth that Jesus is God. Myrrh is a sweet-smelling substance that was used to prepare dead bodies. It traditionally represents Christ's humanity because Jesus, even though he was God, lived as a human and died a human death.

The Flight to Egypt (10 minutes)

Supplies: Bibles, whiteboard or large sheet of paper, markers

While we celebrate the visit of the magi in Christmas pageants and decorations, the story of the magi in the Bible goes along with one of the most tragic stories in all of scripture.

Discuss:

- Who or what are the magi looking for?
- Whom do they go to first?
- How did King Herod react to the magi's visit?

A participant should read aloud the following:

> *King Herod considered Jesus a threat to his power and authority. He responded to this threat in the most brutal way imaginable.*

A participant should read aloud Matthew 2:13-18.
Discuss:

- How did Herod respond to the possibility of a new king?
- How did Jesus and his family respond to Herod's plot?

Jesus and his family moved to a foreign land because their lives were in jeopardy. Think of situations in today's world that might cause a family to move to another country or city, or completely change their way of life. Examples might include fleeing a civil war or government oppression, moving to a bigger city to get medical treatment, and so forth. List any examples you come up with on a whiteboard or large sheet of paper.

Once you have a pretty good list, spend time in prayer for all the people whose lives have been altered by violence, sickness, or uncertainty. Begin by spending a moment in silent prayer. Then a participant should read aloud each item on your list, one at a time. After each item is read, the group should respond, "Lord, hear our prayer." Close with another time of silent prayer.

He Is *the* Lord, but Is He *Your* Lord? (10–15 minutes)

Supplies: pens or pencils

Discuss:

- One of the most common titles given to Jesus is *Lord*. What does it mean to refer to Jesus as Lord?
- What is a "lord" and how does that title relate to Christ?

A participant should read aloud the following:

> *A lord is a person in charge of a particular area or realm. A lord could be a king, a governor, a mayor, an owner of a large estate with many workers, or the head of a clan or family. The lord is responsible for collecting and distributing resources, such as food. When we refer to Jesus as our Lord, we are saying that Jesus is our leader, the one in charge. We honor his authority and look to him for protection and to provide for our needs.*

Divide into teams of three or four. Teams should work together to complete the sentences below.

- Jesus, our Lord, protects us by . . .

- Jesus, our Lord, provides for us by . . .

- Jesus, our Lord, instructs us to . . .

- We serve Jesus, our Lord, by . . .

Teams should work for about five minutes. Then each team should read aloud its sentences.

Discuss:

- How do our lives change when we recognize Jesus as our Lord?
- What other "lords" compete for our loyalty and keep us from following Jesus? (Consider not only human leaders, but also other things that would distract us from our relationship with Jesus.)

Closing (5–10 minutes)

Discuss:

- What is one thing you learned during our time together that you didn't know before?
- What is one thing that you will do in the coming week as a result of what we learned or discussed? (Think especially about the examples you listed during the final activity.)

Then close with the following prayer or one of your choosing:

Lord, thank you again for this time we've had to learn from scripture and from one another. As we move on from this Advent and Christmas season, equip and empower us to live as your disciples, looking to you for guidance and protection. We pray all these things in the name of Jesus Christ, our Lord. Amen.